D1525878

PARADISE AND PIRATES:
Key West The Way It Was

PARADISE AND PIRATES:
Key West The Way It Was

KEITH TERRACINA

EDITING AND PUBLISHING BY MAX ZAHNER

CONTENTS

PROLOGUE: THIS IS PARADISE

considered myself a Conch in 1976. That's when I became a part of Key West, a true local. But Key West became a part of me on my first trip there back in 1969 at the impressionable age of 13.

I'd heard stories about my grandfather, Anthony "Captain Tony" Tarracino. He'd sent pictures—many taken by my Great Uncle Sal—and other gifts so I felt like I already knew him when my family took a two week vacation to sunny Florida. We spent a week in Miami with my father's mobster buddies who'd retired there and then Captain Tony chartered a Cessna for us to see him in Key West.

Growing up in Elizabeth, New Jersey, Miami had been unlike anything I'd ever seen before but it didn't prepare me for the paradise that awaited. From the air I marveled at the turquoise water and the swaying palm trees as we made our approach for landing. Stepping onto the tarmac I finally laid eyes on my grandfather.

There on the runway stood Captain Tony next to his station wagon with his face painted on the doors and a giant fish mounted on top—a rolling billboard for his fishing charter .

*Capitan Tony with Sombo one of Tennessee Williams famous monkeys in front of
Tony's Cadillac.*

The family piled into the wagon and Captain Tony
chauffeured us through the streets of Key West for a brief
tour on the way to the Howard Johnson's to drop off our
luggage. We swung by his house where we met his third
wife and my grandfather's stepkids with whom I'd soon be
riding bicycles, exploring the dirt roads and back alleys of
the island. I was quickly falling in love with Key West and we
hadn't even made it to my grandfather's bar, yet. That was
the next stop on the tour.

Rolling up in front of Captain Tony's Saloon was a surreal
experience. I stood awestruck on the sidewalk. The sound
of screaming monkeys, legendary Key West bongo band the
Junkanoos banging away, and an acid rock band tuning up

echoing out to the street only hinted at the exotic world that awaited me inside .

Capitan Tony's saloon 1964 before the wall was removed and floor excavated to make the pool room.

Stepping through the doors was like an LSD trip. The walls were decorated like an eclectic museum: papier mache masks, celebrity photos, cannon balls, giant taxidermied sharks. Most captivating to my 13-year-old eyes were the busty barmaids in see-through t-shirts. Captain Tony was a showman who knew how to sell the sizzle; whether it was a boat trip on his 65-foot party boat or a bar, he hooked you and reeled you in. If I'd had any doubts that this was paradise, they had been completely dashed.

The rest of the trip reaffirmed my fascination with my grandfather and Key West. He took us to one of the island's premier seafood restaurants. As we walked up the steps, everyone was shaking his hand like he was a celebrity or a wise guy in his dress pants, Italian knit shirt, and bare feet. The attention continued throughout the meal.

My third grandmother didn't join us for dinner but Captain Tony's beautiful blonde girlfriend did. I began to realize there were a lot of differences not just between Key West and New Jersey, but also the world as I knew it. I had a lot to learn about life and I wanted to learn it in Key West.

The vacation ended much too soon and I returned to my drab existence up north with treasured memories and a newfound hope. I now had a mission: I was going to find my way back to Key West.

Key West wasn't the way it was because of Capitan Tony but Key West wouldn't be what it is today if not for his legacy.

1

A JERSEY BOY HEADS SOUTH

As a kid, tales of my grandfather had fueled my imagination. Before he became Captain Tony, he was already a larger-than-life character with mob connections back in New Jersey. Tony Tarracino learned how to hustle on the streets of Elizabeth, New Jersey, where he ran with the mob in the 1940s. Back then, the city was a hotbed of mafia activity, though it flew under the radar compared to places like New York City or Chicago. Tony and his older brother Sal were real mobster types—cunning, reckless, and always on the lookout

1934 The Elizabeth New Jersey gangster turned Capitan who became the Last Pirate and then Mayor emeritus Tony Terracino.

for a good score. Sal had a creative side, too. He was an aspiring photographer and professional pianist which allowed him to move freely throughout the artistic circles.

In 1947, televisions were becoming popular. The technology was so new that manipulating antennas to find a channel and lock in a picture was a combination of technical know-how and sorcery. You could sometimes conjure up a radio signal on the TV and vice versa. This extended to radio signals that weren't even intended for public broadcast. Tony and his brother found someone who could get the live results from a racetrack over the airwaves, allowing them to lay down bets with bookies who were none the wiser. That was a pretty good scam for a short time.

Another enterprise for the Tarracinos and their buddies was procuring merchandise from the Newark docks and re-selling it. Some of the owners of that merchandise were not the type to report the theft to the police, possibly because not all of their business dealings were strictly legal, either. Ripping off bookies and "shopping" at the docks were just a couple of Tony's activities that put him in debt to people who used tactics intended to strongly encourage prompt payment.

By the end of 1947, Tony had two contracts out on him, not to kill him, just to recover the money. He was kidnapped and taken to the Jersey City dumps. The beating he received there knocked out a couple teeth, broke some ribs, blackened an eye, and gave him a concussion. This was not the end of his trouble; there were still plenty of other wise guys who wanted a piece of Tony Tarracino.

1934 Sal Terracina the world traveled master mentalist, psychic, visionary, artist and photographer taken by himself.

Sal may have been more of a character than his little brother, Tony. He was an aspiring photographer, a professional pianist the world's youngest mind reader, and he worked for Frank Castello during Prohibition. His array of talents opened doors to many social and artistic circles. So did being gay. One of his closest friends was the playwright Tennessee Williams.

Long before Tony's underground entrepreneurship had begun catching up with him, Tennessee had been telling Sal that Key West was a hideaway paradise. Even though it had some high profile visitors and residents like Ernest Hemingway, it was an island where someone could be gay and wild without a care in the world. Tony wasn't gay but after the beating he'd taken, he thought Florida sounded like a nice change of pace.

Tony packed up the car and slipped out of town with his soon-to-be second wife, Mae. He had enough cash from his Jersey hustles that they got a room in a fancy Miami hotel on the way to the Keys. Unfortunately, my grandfather was also a degenerate gambler and the lure of the dog racing tracks was irresistible. Within three weeks he'd squandered all his money, sold his car, and sent his girlfriend back north.

Hitchhiking down to Key West seemed like Tony's only option. Once there, he looked for a friend that Tennessee had mentioned but he wasn't around. Within days, my grandfather was homeless and living under the docks with Key West's transients: the dock rats. Eventually he got a job "heading" shrimp for 20 cents a bucket at the Singleton Fish House, part of the 1940s "pink gold" rush when shrimp beds were discovered in the waters of Key West. Tony didn't know how brutal the spines on the shrimp heads could be on his hands. The pain and swelling diminished as he learned the technique of his more experienced co-workers but he was anxious to gain other employment.

From humble beginnings as an ice house and morgue the old hanging tree is the only constant throughout the centuries.

Tony wasn't usually a drinker but he knew that hanging out in bars—including the original Hemingway bar which was the Duval Club— was the best way to connect with any locals who might line him up with a better job. Fortunately, he was very nautical. With his knowledge of tides and fishing, he talked his way onto fishing crews where he learned shrimping and the finer points of fishing around Key West and Cuba. Within a year and a half he was officially a first mate on one of Mr. Paul's two fishing boats. If you're familiar with Mrs Paul's fish sticks, this was her husband. He took a liking to my grandfather and asked him to become a partner and captain one of the boats. It would have been a multimillion dollar opportunity but he wanted to be his own person. He saved enough money to buy his own boat—

christened the Greyhound—and became Captain Tony.

Never one to think small, the new captain had visions of building the largest charter fishing operation in the Keys. The Italian from Jersey brought a fast-talking bravado to drum up business that aggravated some of the local fishing captains. He didn't care—he knew how to reel the tourists in. He'd mastered the Cuban-style handline fishing techniques and knew how to put customers on big game like goliath grouper and yellowtail. At night, he'd entertain passengers with tales of his past life in the mob.

1965 Captain Tony catches a world record 14 foot tiger shark and poses with his daughters Coral and Toni

Business was booming in no time. The successive Greyhound II and Greyhound III were bigger and more elaborate, featuring turbocharged diesel engines. And business was not limited to rods and reels. It was supplemented by the sale of booze on the upper deck bars by lovely "bartenders" who doubled as wet t-shirt contestants. The clientele knew that Captain Tony could take them to the best fishing spots while throwing the best parties in the Keys.

In his many stints as an apprentice crewman, Captain Tony had also learned the smuggling trade. While he occasionally hauled rubber and sponges, Cuban rum was much more lucrative contraband. When CIA agents started coming around asking for Tony's help running spies into Cuba, he was happy to oblige—for the right price. The cloak-and-dagger work reached its peak during the lead-up to the failed Bay of Pigs invasion in 1961. The Greyhound III transported CIA-trained Cuban exiles for secret missions. Rumor has it Captain Tony was even involved in a plot to assassinate Fidel Castro, though few details can be verified.

The infamous Greyhound IV. 65ft dual turbo diesel duel deck fishing boat that also ran moonlight "supply" trips to Cuba

Some of the profits from these ventures went back into the business, like upgrading boats and painting Captain Tony's face on the side of a station wagon. But Captain Tony was not accumulating wealth. He was still a gambler and the greyhounds and other games of chance siphoned off plenty of funds. One bet that supposedly paid off, though, was a high-stakes poker game around 1964. At least that's the most popular of the many colorful, conflicting, and likely apocryphal stories about how Tony Tarracino acquired what became the iconic Captain Tony's Saloon. Regardless of how it fell into his hands, Tony relished the opportunity to put his mark on Key West's oldest original bar.

The humble, dusty, and dirty white building had once served as both an ice house and a morgue. According to legend, a sprawling live oak tree in the back had been the site of over 50 hangings in the 19th century. With a history like that, no wonder the place was said to be haunted!

Tony embraced the saloon's checkered past. He hung the taxidermied sharks from the rafters, installed a complete human skeleton behind the bar that is still on display today, and let a pair of Tennessee Williams' creepy and energetic capuchin monkeys Sambo and Creature take up residence in a giant cage surrounding the hanging tree. Businessmen, smugglers, eccentric artists and bohemian types were drawn to the bar's ramshackle vibe. In addition to a rotation of house bands like the renowned Junkanoos and their bongos, it was common to see the reggae Pacific Orchestra or Jimmy Buffett play late into the night with impromptu jam sessions. Buffett name-checked his good friend's saloon in multiple song lyrics, such as "The Last Mango in Paris," which famously has the original handwritten lyrics framed in the Men's room, helping cement its reputation as the quintessential Key West hangout .

Already a famous photographer from New York, Tony's brother Sal helped cement the saloon's reputation when he started spending winters in Key West. Sal set up a studio above the bar where he shot eerie avant-garde portraits. He also hosted wild private parties fueled by booze, music, and his handcrafted masks. Sal's gay lifestyle flourished in Key West's open-minded and permissive environment. Through him, Tony's bar became a hangout for many prominent gay men of the era.

By then, Sal's old friend Tennessee Williams owned a house on the island. Tennessee introduced his literary pals like Truman Capote and Shel Silverstein to Tony's saloon. Conversations in the corner booth could range from keen artistic insight to unrestrained and bawdy humor.

Local newspapers chronicled visits by other celebrities over the years, including heavyweight champion Muhammad Ali. His bodyguards had heard Key West had the best fishing so he was at the docks looking for a charter. As he passed Captain Tony's slip my grandfather proclaimed to the champ, "Come on my boat 'cause it's the greatest!"

That was the Key West that I'd gotten a small taste of in 1969.

2

DISCOVERING PARADISE

Elizabeth, New Jersey, was a gritty blue collar town dominated by smoke-belching factories and congested highways packed with honking cars. The Jersey Shore resorts where Italians like my family vacationed every summer were light years away from Key West. That's what I'd learned back in 1969 .

The Terracina family on vacation in Miami Beach on their way to Key West. 1969.

My memory of that magical trip seemed like a fever dream. Wandering the backstreets of Key West on a bike, I'd soaked up the island's intoxicating atmosphere those first few days. I was enthralled listening to tall tales from old salts at the harbor, watching a street artist named Monkey Tom dash off a seaside sunset scene on a hubcap in mere minutes. Kerry, one of Captain Tony's stepkids, had been my guide to this sun-drenched paradise. Just a year older than me, Kerry provided my first taste of the special camaraderie formed among those lured to Key West by wanderlust and the romance of the open sea.

Together Kerry and I explored back alleys echoing with melodic Cuban voices, scrutinized the cemetery's above-ground tombs with their neo-Gothic frills, and plucked spiny sea urchins from tide pools. We marveled at the strange flora, sniffed fragrant frangipani blossoms, and crushed leathery sea grape leaves between our fingers. I'll never forget watching the colors spread across the sky as the sun sank behind Mallory square, while a few local musicians played their last few melodies of the day .

Bongo players at Mallory Square and their biggest fan set the scene as the crowd gathers for another sunset celebration

I was not the only one who'd been enchanted by the island's allure. My dad, Lou, felt the same pull; following in Captain Tony's footsteps he moved to Key West in the early '70s. This was not out of character for him. Before splitting when I was 15, he was always hatching harebrained schemes to make a quick buck and live large. Like the time he stole a truckload of new TVs and carpets, selling the hot merchandise on the sly to furnish our house and half the neighborhood. Lou ran painting and construction scams, squandering the profits constantly upgrading our rides and taking us on lavish vacations. For all his faults, Lou knew how to live it up when his scams paid off.

Of course, Lou's high times never lasted for long before he overplayed his hand, forcing us to lie low for a while. But there were moments of pure joy I'll never forget, like one special family trip to the Jersey Shore. After winning big at the poker tables all week, my uncles tried to prank Lou but he ended up winning a brand new Cadillac in a boardwalk raffle. Everyone roared as Lou chased his brothers up and down the block in celebration.

For a couple of years, our little family really lived the *Goodfellas* life thanks to Lou's illicit activities. He treated the whole neighborhood to sleigh rides and dinners out, winning Dad of the Year from the Boy Scouts, of all people. Then a year after the big Key West trip, it all evaporated when Lou left us for a woman named Peggy. Just like his idol and father, Captain Tony, Lou was incapable of domestic bliss. He ran away with his new girlfriend to Las Vegas for 6 months and then Ft. Meyers beach for 6 more months before Captain Tony convinced him to buy a boat and move to Key West. I took it hard, losing my hero and partner-in-crime. I started down a darker path in Jersey and started running my own scams and experimenting with LSD.

Thoughts of Key West continued to consume my adolescent dreams. The mundane rhythms of high school and my dead-end town bored me. I yearned to return to that balmy island where adventure lurked around every corner. A few years later, at the age of 16, I finally worked up the nerve to run away to my dad's place in Ft. Meyer's

Beach. But the brief idyll ended with a juvenile detention stay that definitely had not been part of the plan. I had to bide my time a little longer before making my escape.

By 1975 I'd secured a civil service job as an exterminator and apartment inspector for the housing authority in Elizabeth. As the owner and operator of ECA Exterminating Corporation of America I was making great money, had a nice car, and lived in an apartment with a stripper. Not a bad life for a 19 year-old guy with no formal training or higher education. In the summer of 1976 I took a week off to go visit my father again who was now settled down in Key West. By the second day there I had full blown Key West fever. Moving there was no longer a dream—it was my destiny .

Keith Terracina, Sal Terracina & little Louie at Truman & Francis, across from Big Daddies, 1976 photo by Tony Tarracino

PARADISE AND PIRATES:
KEY WEST THE WAY IT WAS

Back in Jersey, it only took me two months to close up shop and convince my friends Joe and Donnie to join me for a week or two in paradise. "You've never seen a place like Key West!" I promised as we packed up Donnie's van with everything I hadn't sold or given away. For them, it was a cheap vacation; for me, it was a new beginning.

The three of us had been friends since childhood. We cruised along the eastern seaboard, reminiscing about our delinquent past and envisioning the new adventures that awaited us in Key West. When we arrived after the long drive, my father welcomed me with open arms. He was thrilled I was moving down to be closer to him. I gave him a hug and put my suitcase in the spare room. When he walked me through the house he had drugs all over the kitchen so we did a sampling before heading to my grandfather's bar to pay our respects. That was my first taste of pure Key West cocaine.

I stayed with Lou those first few weeks as my two buddies and I took in the local scene. We explored the palm tree-lined streets on bicycles and dove into the crystalline waters of the Gulf. The pace of life was slower, more relaxed than the hustle of Jersey.

After a few weeks of paradise, it was time for Donnie and Joe to head home. But by now Donnie had succumbed to the island's magnetic pull: he had Key West fever, too. "Keith, this place is too good to give up," he confessed. "I'm not going back." True to his word, Donnie never left of his own volition. He became a local legend, starting a business renting rafts to tourists near the beach.

I moved from my dad's house into an apartment in a house overlooking the old cemetery thanks to a friendly hippie landlord who skipped town and left me his place. I grew accustomed to the strange sounds that drifted in through my open windows at night. I started settling in, and getting to know the local restaurant owners and bartenders. Key West welcomed me with open arms.

My dream had come true.

3

SETTLING INTO ISLAND LIFE

C aptain Tony's Saloon in 1976 was just as mesmerizing as it had been when I first visited seven years earlier. Pacific Orchestra was playing reggae and everyone was ready to party. Rusty mines and anchors littered the walk out front. Inside, Sambo and Creature were no longer in residence, but there was a cackling mynah bird and the ever-present buxom bartenders in skimpy Captain Tony's Saloon t-shirts. The joint reeked gloriously of spilled beer, coconut suntan oil, and marijuana smoke. Captain Tony welcomed me back .

1979 Metro lights up the Capitan Tony's Saloon dancefloor with New Wave rock 'n' roll.

It didn't take long for me to feel right at home in Key West. Surrounded by mentors like my grandfather Captain Tony and my dad who introduced me to his eccentric neighbors and friends, real Key West characters each one: smugglers, dealers, hustlers, gangsters, and some just run-of-the-mill quirky Conchs. Lou jokingly warned me that Key West might be too wild for a kid like me, but I wasn't about to listen. Paradise had its dangers, but I had street smarts and resilience.

Donnie secured a night watchman job at Billy's Bar on Front Street, which turned into our own private after-hours club that we called Donnie's. He'd stay down there while working days renting out rafts to tourists, eventually becoming known as "Double Raft Donnie." As for me, I started crewing on fishing boats, working my way up to first mate.

Key West is famous for many things. But since it's a tiny two-by-three-mile island surrounded by the Atlantic Ocean and the Gulf of Mexico, the incredible snorkeling, diving, sailing, and variety of fishing options make it a world-class water sports destination. My dad's best friend, Captain Andy Griffith Sr., had a lobster and stone crab boat and a commercial fishing boat to work the reef in all seasons. I started on his lobster boat pulling the 800 traps he had scattered across many square miles of ocean.

Captain Andy was up on the flying bridge, navigating to each string's buoy. I was down with the winch, pulling up the string of traps, gaffing each trap to pull it on board, taking out the lobsters, leaving the baby lobsters, cleaning the trap, changing the bait, and pushing the trap back into the ocean before gaffing the next trap on the string. Each string had about 20 traps and the whole process had to be executed for every trap in under four minutes. That was all day for three straight days .

1981, Lou Terracina(R) Captain Andy Griffith Sr(M) Andy Jr(L). After 8 hours of reeling in Kingfish by Keith Terracina.

Even better were the 10-day runs out to the Dry Tortugas. We'd load up with at least a ton of ice, and extra fuel tanks, and head out to catch hundreds of pounds of yellowtail, grouper, and snapper with handlining—we had bicycle innertubes on our hands for protection—from sun down to sun up every day. The mornings were spent gutting fish and filling the refrigerator-sized ice chests with our haul. I ended up working with several crews, but it was with Captain

Andy that I truly learned my skills and proved my worth. I worked my ass off and loved it.

That time at sea was just what I needed to clear my head after too much hardcore partying. After every trip, I'd return to shore with a lot of cash and dive back into Key West's wicked nightlife of debauchery fueled by alcohol, weed, quaaludes, and top-shelf cocaine. The island had a lot more to offer than water sports.

Since the 1960s—and probably even during its pirate days—Key West had been a very sexual resort. The gay community could always be pretty wild but visitors emerged from lots of other closets, too. I saw it hundreds of times: people felt uninhibited in mystical Key West. Gay men would hold hands and flirt openly before it became commonplace elsewhere in the States. It was almost like that freedom gave license for everyone to cut loose and experiment. There was always an orgy to be found and any fetish could be satisfied. An evening might start with alcohol and skinny dipping but the high-quality drugs and the permissive atmosphere usually escalated the festivities.

That's not to say there wasn't any resistance to alternative lifestyles in Key West. For a while in the 1960s and 1970s, there was a ride-along program where a gay man would partner with a patrol officer in his car for a shift to monitor police. Some of the officers had joined—or at least turned a blind eye to—locals in harassment of patrons of Key West's biggest gay bar.

There were about a dozen prostitutes who worked downtown Key West in the 1970s. Two of them were cross-dressing men. They'd approach a tourist or a serviceman and offer their services. A walk by the pier would lead to oral gratification under the pier. Bree was the master at working a guy at the bar: get them to buy him a drink, kiss him on the ear, slide a hand into his lap, maybe grab just enough to show this was more than flirting. The mark wouldn't even realize he was heading into the alley with a man. Sometimes a bartender or the manager would tell the guy's buddies what was going on. He'd come back in with a big grin, bragging about getting some action, only to have his buddies razz him mercilessly.

Captain Tony's wasn't a gay bar. It cast its net so wide that it was hard to define its clientele. But gay men definitely could find a good time there. Tennessee Williams and Truman Capote were frequent visitors when Sal was in town. At 20 years old, I had no idea who either of them were. One night I'm working at the bar and a cab rolls up with two guys wrapped in sheets like togas. My grandfather greets the older one with a hug and a kiss on the cheek. I asked the saloon's manager, Peter, who these guys were and he brought me up to speed: it was Tennessee Williams and his boyfriend.

Plenty of patrons in the bar already recognized the playwright before he reached the bar. It got a little frenzied for a bit as people pressed in for autographs or to bend his ear. I guess meeting a great storyteller inspires people to share their own.

My grandfather introduced me to Tennessee who responded with shock.

"Oh, my God, I can't believe you have a grandson!"

I guess when Captain Tony regaled people with tales of his past, there wasn't much focus on domestic life.

Tennessee peppered me with questions. Did I miss Jersey? What did I think of Key West? Anything interesting happen at sea?

Great storytellers are also great listeners.

Sal's Papier-mâché mix had Acid, Haitian voodoo dust, pyramid scrapings from Egypt and some wild potions from Cambodia.

A couple weeks later Tennessee dropped by the saloon to visit Sal who was up in his studio loft where he crafted hand-painted papier mache and plaster masks. Tennessee went upstairs with my grandfather and I followed. They'd all known each other for over 30 years. I sat fascinated as they discussed Sal's masks and portraits and the different irons that each of them had in the fire. They finally turned their attention in my direction, teasing me about *not* being gay and my success at picking up girls. Sometimes the topics would get pretty heavy and it was obvious that they were dear friends who could talk about anything.

Hanging out at Captain Tony's Saloon there was always a chance a celebrity might drop by: Tennessee would show up with Paul Lynde or Truman Capote. One day this colorful bus rolls up and my grandfather gives a firm handshake and gets a kiss on the cheek from this sandy-haired beach bum-looking guy who steps off. Just like with Tennessee Williams, people start pressing in. Captain Tony waves them off and signals me to come over with a tilt of his head.

"I want you to meet someone."

That's how I met Jimmy Buffett. He was also amazed that Captain Tony had a grandson. It didn't fit with my 59-year-old grandfather's persona as a carefree player. Hell, it didn't fit when he was an 89-year-old player .

1979 Spring Break while Big twist and the Mellow Fellows are on stage Jimmy Buffet strolls in to jam a few tunes.

Jimmy invited us on the bus and we cruised down Greene Street to Simonton. I assumed we were headed to the beach. Jimmy asked me what I thought of island life. I told him it was really cool. Then he asked me what I thought of his music.

Some of Buffett's "island music" was on the jukebox but I found it annoying. I was into rock: Grand Funk Railroad, Jimi Hendrix, Deep Purple, Led Zeppelin. I admitted that I wasn't too impressed with his songs. He laughed. We've talked about that conversation many times. He appreciated my honesty and I've since grown to appreciate his style.

One of Jimmy's crew lit up a joint and started passing it around. Jimmy took a hit and eventually, it got to my grandfather. That was the first time I ever saw him smoke weed. He wasn't a drinker so I suspected he had to be doing something else. Now I finally knew his occasional drug of choice. We never got to the beach. We just drove around—even passing the saloon a few times—until most of us were really stoned and then we got dropped off back at the bar. Just another day in paradise.

Fashion designer Calvin Klein would pop into Captain Tony's to say hi to my grandfather and Sal. His house on Eaton Street was the most expensive on the island. He invited Sal to one of his lavish parties there and I convinced Sal to take me along. I got as dressed up as my wardrobe and sensibilities would allow. I'm not sure what I was expecting but even by Key West standards it was a wild affair. There were a bunch of breathtaking women—as I'd hoped—and about 80 gay young men—as I'd expected. That night really opened my eyes to gay culture. I'd only been on the periphery of it in Key West, and of course, back in Jersey, my homophobia had been ingrained. This was the first time I really had long conversations with gay guys my age. Turns out they were regular guys and they *really* knew how to party. I did leave the soirée early to go back to Captain Tony's Saloon to finish off the night. I left Sal behind. He was in heaven.

While Calvin Klein's parties were epic, it didn't take much to throw a party in Key West. With all the drunk or high people concentrated on a little island, any group of people was on the cusp of critical mass for a party to break out—or a fight. There were a few rough areas on the island.

1979 Spring Break while Big twist and the Mellow Fellows are on stage Jimmy Buffet strolls in to jam a few tunes.

My dad and Captain Tony had offered me guidance when I was new in town. They warned me to avoid Duval and Fleming after dark, where the West Key Bar and Boat Bar attracted rough crowds—violent drunken brawls and topless women dancing on the bar were common. Still, if you were looking for the real Key West, those were the most interesting dives on the island . Every bar, restaurant, and club had its own unique personality and stories. From the rowdy all-night Boca Chica Lounge on Stock Island to The Jungle Room where my granddad made deals, The Bull where I got strong drinks after closing Captain Tony's, and

38

Sugarloaf Lodge, which was a haven for dealers from up North.

Original glass slides of my great uncle Sal's collection, Sloppy Joe's 2nd location from the early 1970s.

For a taste of luxury, there was The Chart Room, Top of the La Concha Hotel, and The Pier House. Historic Sloppy Joe's (not the original location) and Rick's Bars were tourist bars but obligatory stops. If I wanted to relax, Mallory Square was the place to go since it welcomed everyone— tourists, locals, families, and even the homeless who camped on nearby boats at night. In the day, you'd find colorful Key West characters plying their trades: Artists, Banana Bread Man, Cookie Lady, Conch Salad Man peddling his raw seafood ceviche from a five-gallon bucket, street artist Monkey Tom with his hubcaps, and more. And I'd get free Cuban meals at El Cacique for directing patrons their way when I worked at Captain Tony's.

Get your Oooey goooyee choooclate chip cooookies! The cookie lady and her sweet treats were staples of Mallory Square

Paintings by the legendary street artist Monkey Tom in the saloon. Photo by Sal Terracina.

What's funny to me now is that I don't remember any iguanas in Key West. Then Iguana Man showed up in Mallory Square and people started taking pictures with his iguana on their shoulder. Apparently, he had at least two iguanas and they mated because now it's like Jurassic Park on the island. They're everywhere. Same with chickens. There used to only be chickens in a few people's backyards. Now there might be more chickens than iguanas .

The iguana man of Key West on the set of Cuban Crossings in 1979. Back then these were the only iguanas in the keys.

Mallory Square was where the action was at sunset, too. But my hippie friends and I preferred the end of Simonton Street with its pier jutting out into the clear Gulf water. I'd swim out to the buoy and back every day to stay in shape.

We respected the families but didn't hide our pot smoking or occasional skinny dipping either. Yeah, I took to the lifestyle like a fish to water, no longer rushing anywhere or worrying about trivial things. We were living on "Key West Time."

Even today, Key West draws all types of creatives: artists, writers, and people with a unique medium for expressing themselves. Not everyone's famous and many never will be. But the island is their muse. There's inspiration around every corner: in the flowers, the palm trees, even the other people. I don't know what it is about this speck of dirt in the middle of the ocean that makes sunsets so beautiful and fascinating; part of me wants to capture each one.

I'd been in Key West for about a year when my father showed me a brand new Nikon camera outfit he'd found: three lenses, a flash, beautiful leather bag, tripod, the whole kit. Someone had stolen it and dumped it on a construction site. For some reason, I thought it'd be cool to walk around with an expensive camera. I needed a hobby besides smoking weed, doing coke, and chasing girls. I gave my father $50 and became a photographer.

I didn't know anything about cameras or photography. I couldn't change the lenses or even load the film. Sal wasn't around that time a year—he was at his New York studio—so I went to the camera store. The owner gave me a quick camera lesson covering basics like shutter speed, aperture, and of course loading film. I bought a few rolls of 100 speed Kodak film, hung the camera around my neck, put the bag over my shoulder, and rode my bicycle down to Captain Tony's Saloon.

As soon as I walked through the door my grandfather exclaimed, "What the hell are you doing?" I recounted my afternoon and he nodded, "That's cool." He'd also done some photography back in Jersey. He wasn't in Sal's league but he could appreciate the appeal.

I walked down to Simonton Street, using up an entire roll taking pictures of the pier and the people and the boats. It felt almost spiritual. After hanging out back at Captain Tony's, I popped in another roll and went to watch the sunset at Mallory Square. I put the big lens on and snapped away as the sun melted into the horizon. I finished off the roll with shots of people and sailboats, having no idea if any of the photos would be any good.

*Sunrise and sunsets taken from Mallory Square, White St Pier and the local's spot,
Simonton st Pier by Keith West 1981*

The next day I dropped off the film, anxious to see the results of my first foray into photography. Four hours later when I picked up that envelope stuffed with glossy prints, I was awed by the beauty of the sunset. Thanks to that very expensive Nikon—it was worth a lot more than $50—I had discovered I could be a photographer. Everything was in focus, not just on the prints but also in my mind. I had visions of creating postcards, posters, and art.

Summers back then were peaceful in Key West. There were hardly any tourists, if any. Captain Tony's only had a band on weekends. On the busiest weekday you might find nine people in the bar listening to the jukebox. The vibe was totally different from the raucous tourist season. I savored the peaceful bicycle rides at night. That was the Key West I tried to capture on film.

I'd go to a deserted Mallory Square at 10 o'clock at night. Even the smell was tranquil. I'd arrive at White Street Pier—the "unfinished highway to Havana"—before dawn and wait for the sunrise. Maybe there'd be a lone fisherman or someone walking their dog but at least a hundred times it was just me and that Nikon. Without it, I might not believe some of these memories.

4

WORKING THE DOOR AT CAPTAIN TONY'S

One night I met a girl at the bar who'd bought four houses on Olivia Street. Her plan was to remodel them and turn them into rental properties. She started dating me because I had connections. Between being Captain Tony's grandson and my experience back in Jersey, I knew people and got things done.

I lined up carpenters and contractors, oversaw demolition, secured building materials. Eventually I moved into one of the houses with her and we had a pretty successful enterprise going. Captain Tony noticed and was impressed that a 21 year-old was so organized and could handle people the way I did. He'd never had a relative work for him, not even my dad, but he thought I was just what he needed at Captain Tony's Saloon.

The Capitan Tony's crew 71-73. Sal's sign advertising his nightly performance can be seen above the door.

The raucous joint could be a challenge but Captain Tony's longtime right-hand man and protégé, Peter, had decided to move on to greener pastures in Miami and my grandfather was in need of someone new to help manage the bar, watch the front door, keep order inside, and collect cash for him at the end of the night. Most importantly, he needed me to toss out any troublemakers. He asked me if I could handle that.

Sure, I could.

In 1977—I'd only been in Key West a year and a half and was barely old enough to drink myself—I was given the prestigious job of running the infamous saloon. Having grown up in the rougher parts of Jersey, I'd hung around mob joints since I was a teenager and figured I could handle just about anything Key West could throw at me. Of course, I was dead wrong.

My trial by fire came during my very first week holding down the fort. Pacific Orchestra was in top form and the place was packed to the rafters with an eclectic mix of sunburned tourists, bearded fishermen, revved-up bikers, and quite a few Cuban locals. To top it off, the large amount of quaaludes and cocaine being passed around meant tensions were running high.

In the corner by the four pool tables, a heated argument erupted between a drunk shrimper built like a silverback gorilla and a skinny long-haired hippie barely half his size. Voices were raised, fingers were pointed, and the two looked about ready to come to blows. Naively thinking I could talk some reason into them, I rushed over and tried to play the diplomat. However, just as I stepped between the quarreling men, the hippie took a wild, telegraphed swing, which I mistakenly thought was aimed at me.

Acting purely on instinct, I grabbed the skinny kid by his shirt collar and slammed him up against the wall, barking at him to knock it off. This caught the big fisherman by surprise, and he reflexively threw a roundhouse haymaker which connected flush to my nose. I saw stars for a moment and felt the warm gush of blood pouring down my face as I crumpled to the ground. Though the shrimp boat captain felt bad and tried to apologize once he realized his error, the damage was done. My pride hurt more than my shattered schnoz, I tossed them both out on their asses and called it a night.

The broken beak was a harsh lesson about reading body language and not jumping into frays I didn't fully understand. Over the following weeks and months at Captain Tony's door, I became an expert at spotting trouble brewing from a mile away. Whether it was muscle tension, hand gestures, the thousand-yard stare, or slurred curses, I learned to trust my gut and defuse problems before they could conflagrate into bar-clearing brawls. De-escalation became my specialty.

Of course, some characters made keeping the peace at Tony's an acute challenge. First and foremost was the notorious Key West Helen, a mentally ill townie who had been 86'd from nearly every drinking establishment for her drunken, abusive antics. The cops usually looked the other way when it came to Helen's misdemeanors, as she was difficult to control and usually ended up right back on the streets after a night in the county jail.

In my early days running the door at Captain Tony's, Helen decided to give me a proper hazing. She looked me in the eye and asked, "Are you the new jerk-off watching the door?"

She catcalled, stumbling up the sidewalk with a bottle in hand, telling me I couldn't do shit to her. Before I could respond, she spit right in my face. As I stood there stunned, wiping the slime from my eyes, Helen got right up in my grill and continued her verbal assault. Just as I was carefully reaching around to stash the cash from the door in my back pocket, Helen took the opportunity to sucker punch me in the nose.

My recently healed schnoz exploded in a crimson torrent once again. Enraged, I instinctively grabbed Helen by her rat's nest hair and slammed her to the pavement. To keep her from squirming away, I put my foot on her stringy mane while yelling for someone to call the cops. Bad optics. An oblivious tourist thought I was some brute beating up his girlfriend—trust me, I was doing *much* better than Helen—so he came running from across the street and tackled me like a linebacker.

I ended up with bruises on top of bruises and a few cracked ribs from the blindside hit. As the well-meaning tourist profusely apologized and helped me up, Helen scurried off into the night cackling. That wild woman would continue to antagonize me outside Tony's for years to come with her drunken verbal assaults, but at least I was wise enough never to lay a hand on her again.

For the most part, business was booming in the late 1970s at Captain Tony's. Word of mouth about the bands and the atmosphere had spread, and tourists flooded the place even during off-peak times. We brought in popular local rock acts to play long sets many nights of the week. To entice the locals, Tony instituted a neighborhood discount with cheap, good drinks. Fishermen, treasure hunters, eccentric artists, and street characters all rubbed elbows at the bar with the locals as equals.

My responsibilities running the door also gave me the opportunity to get to know many of Key West's unique personalities up close and personal. For someone in his early 20s learning the ways of the world, it was an invaluable education that money couldn't buy.

Of course, not all of the bar goers were pleasant eccentrics there just to throw back a few drinks and spin yarns. Plenty were belligerent troublemakers whose only reason for getting plastered was to start fights and harass the female patrons. Tossing these unruly drunks out on their rears often proved a dicey proposition. Slurred threats of bodily harm were common. I usually had to summon backup from a crazy neighbor, Phillip, who smuggled with Captain Tony. He was famous in the Vietnam war for his love of the flamethrower.

Some of the worst offenders were the crews of shrimpers and fishermen back to shore after weeks or months out at sea. Flush with cash in hand, these mariners were eager to blow off steam by imbibing insane amounts of booze and ingesting all available drugs. They would arrogantly dare me at gunpoint, knowing full well that they could overpower me if riled. Luckily, I discovered the right words and firm tone to employ which appealed to their pride and preserved the peace. Very rarely did these confrontations turn physical if handled early with respect.

After months at sea sailors came into port with pockets full of cash and two things on their mind. Tony's satisfied both

The worst troublemaker during my early days in charge was a shrimp fisherman, Larry. Built like a superhero cartoon, his neck and traps bulged wildly, seeming mismatched to his boyish face. Though he looked barely 18, the man was pure muscle from hauling nets and had an alarming strength when drunk and enraged. He put several people in the hospital during his occasional drug-fueled rampages. Bullet Bob, another bouncer, warned me to keep Larry out of Captain Tony's or risk losing our liquor license. Everyone was terrified of the maniac.

Of course, keeping him away completely proved

impossible. Bored with sitting around his room at the flophouse drinking rotgut, he would show up itching for a fight whenever the mood struck. One menacing glare was enough to send most patrons scurrying from his path, but I knew I had to stand my ground. Our first confrontation nearly came to blows when I refused him entry for previous unruly behavior. His buddy tugged him away before he could swing on me.

The next time he darkened our door, I stood tall and looked him straight in the eye with an air of wary understanding. He glared at me for a moment, fists clenched, before nodding begrudgingly and taking a seat by himself in the corner. Crisis averted. Over subsequent weeks, our relationship evolved to one of mutual wariness. I would allow him in as long as he behaved himself, and he refrained from making me his personal punching bag. We avoided a showdown that would have caused great damage to both man and property. Showing his more cultured and less destructive side, he would show up with chess sets during the day to play with girls at the bar and they loved it.

Some of the trouble was harder to spot.

There was a grifter my grandfather called the Fox. He first showed up a few months before I moved to Key West. He'd come in with a few friends and then go over to Captain Tony and chat him up. He was loud and a little annoying but he seemed harmless. He bought lots of drinks for his guests and even tried to buy drinks for the Captain.

By the time I was running the saloon, everyone was used to seeing him pop in occasionally but no one knew anything else about him. One day he called and asked when Captain Tony would be there. I didn't know. The Fox told me to let Captain Tony know he was coming down. When my grandfather did show up I didn't even tell him about the call. Why would he even care?

That evening the Fox shows up with a couple and he leaves them at their table while he talks to Captain Tony. He makes a real show of greeting my grandfather with a hug like they're old friends and introduces him to the couple before telling them he needs to talk to Captain Tony. The Fox follows him to the bar and leans in real close while they talk about fishing for a few minutes. Then he goes back to the table to talk to the couple. After a couple minutes, the Fox nods at Captain Tony and leaves. After he finished his drink, my grandfather did what he did 6 out of 7 nights every week and left for the dog track.

The couple enjoys a few more drinks in the pool room but as the night wears on they're looking increasingly anxious and annoyed. I always studied everyone in the bar so I could anticipate trouble. These two weren't going to start a fight or anything but they were clearly enjoying themselves less and less. The guy finally comes over to ask me when Captain Tony's coming back. I brushed him off with, "Later."

That didn't satisfy him but I didn't want to engage in conversation. He returned to his table in a huff. People who aren't having a good time usually leave if you ignore them and they take their negative energy with them. However, these two weren't leaving.

The guy was getting edgier and kept pestering me every 20 or 30 minutes about Captain Tony. He told me that his friend was with the Fox and they were supposed to all meet back here. That's when I figured something was going down but I had no idea what. My grandfather finally returns and this guy runs up to him and asks where the Fox is.

Captain Tony immediately knew what was going on. The Fox had used him to set these people up.

"I don't know the Fox. He comes in here to drink and chat but we aren't friends and I've never seen him outside these walls."

Now the guy starts to panic.

"What are you talking about? Where's our stuff? What happened to the Fox?"

My grandfather was firm with him.

"I don't know what the hell you're talking about but I don't have any dealings with the Fox and I *never* have anybody's 'stuff'."

That's when I stepped in.

"Listen, I don't know what happened. I don't know who you're dealing with, but *we* don't know what's going on. We're not a part of any deal or transaction."

Now the guy's screaming at his girlfriend—I thought he was going to hit her—because she's the one who'd hooked them up with the Fox. We pieced together that the Fox had promised them that his dear friend Captain Tony would score them the best cocaine of their lives. They just needed to rent a car and bring a bunch of cash to Key West. The meet-and-greet earlier in the evening had all been for show and then the Fox had taken their rental car to their hotel room to get the cash and then go close the deal with Captain Tony, who he knew would leave for the dog track but they would think was meeting up with the Fox. Of course, by now the Fox had probably already reached Miami in their rental and was checking into a beachfront hotel with their cash.

The couple kept pressing us for information on the Fox but there was nothing we could tell them. I'm not sure they believed us. I finally threw them out.

Guess you strolls in about 8 months later? The Fox acted as if nothing had happened. I confronted him before he even got through the door..

"Hey, man, you can't come in here. You put my grandfather in a bad situation."

He said he didn't know what I was talking about and that must have been someone else, not him.

"Well, neither one of you is welcome in Captain Tony's Saloon."

We never saw him again.

Dealing with an endless parade of grifters, hotheads, bullies, and intoxicated lunatics at Captain Tony's every night forced me to mature fast. I learned how to handle the mentally ill and talk people down from irrational rage. One of my tricks was to very quietly tell troublemakers that two undercover cops were casing the place and looking for easy arrests. This made it in everyone's best interest to settle down. Keeping cool under pressure soon became second nature. By the time I turned 22, I could defuse most any bar dustup like a seasoned pro. Running the door at Captain Tony's was an intense trial by fire which engendered confidence and taught me the art of reading people.

Those hard lessons served me well in later pursuits like photography, where I had to put strangers at ease instantly to capture their essence. My time holding down the fort and breaking up brawls at my grandfather's iconic watering hole were formative experiences that made me the man I am today.

I'm sure those scenarios play out every day all over the world but I can't imagine anyplace else had the frequency of chaos and insanity that was a typical day during Key West's peak.

In 1978, a production company sent a producer, Peter J. Barton, to visit Captain Tony. They were looking for a story to turn into a movie starring Miss Germany fourth runner-up Marie-Louise Gassen. Her husband was a millionaire musician and producer from Germany, Jack White, and the only way she was going to get into a movie is if one was written for her. They finally decided to focus on Captain Tony's exploits with the CIA, creating a fictional account of a bitter Cuban who lost everything to Castro and plots to assassinate him.

We didn't really know what was going on when my grandfather said they were making a movie about his life. I thought he'd optioned his life story for a book. Then he showed me the $80,000 check. It got real when he closed the bar for two weeks during filming and crews were shutting down streets for the shoot. I still thought it was just a documentary until actors started showing up along with the film crew.

Mary-Louise didn't even have the lead in her own movie and she never appeared in anything else. That's all you need to know about her acting chops. Playing a Cuban with a broken German accent was not her breakthrough role.

There were a few recognizable faces in the cast like Robert Vaughn, Woody Strode, Sybil Danning, Caren Kaye, and Michael Gazzo who played Rossellini in *The Godfather*. Stuart Whitman played my grandfather, the boat captain transporting the vengeful Cuban exile played by Vaughn. Captain Tony did get a cameo as a Cuban on a horse and there were parts for me and my buddies from Jersey. We were Special Forces guys who came ashore in rafts and got to be stunt men in bar fights or getting killed on the beach.

The whole shoot turned into a party: everyone doing blow, smoking weed, crazy dinners. Whitman and Captain Tony became good friends and left the set for three days with a couple of young tourists. They took the women to

Whitman's condo in Puerto Rico. Barton was furious. So were Captain Tony's wife and girlfriend.

We had a blast but *Cuba Crossing* was a mess. Everything on the screen was awful and it bombed. The end result was a laughably bad film, though it did capture some of the "anything goes" atmosphere of Key West. It was re-released a couple of times as *Assignment - Kill Castro* and *Sweet Dirty Tony*. None of those offerings did any better. The problem wasn't the title.

If I had been paying closer attention, I might have realized that the movie's production and the final result was a cautionary tale on drugs and excess .

Karen on the set of the Captain Tony movie "Cuban Crossings" with Tony's son Lou in the saloon doorway

5

DEALING DRUGS AND DODGING THE LAW

All walks of life came through Capitan Tony's and many of the island's inhabitants took on the pirate traits from the legendary smuggler Captain Tony himself. With weekly card games including prominent Key West figures, the sidewalk Mayor of Key West had more than enough chances to lean his influence on everyone including the infamous Bum Farto, the Fire Chief of Key West who mysteriously disappeared in 1976 while awaiting trial for high profile trafficking charges. His mysterious disappearance akin to Jimmy Hoffa remains one of the island's biggest mysteries to this day with "Where is Bum Farto?" t-shirts still popular.

Of course, actually dealing drugs was illegal, even in laidback Key West. But the cops generally looked the other way as long as it was small-time local stuff that stayed on the island. They were more concerned with smugglers moving product off the island to Miami and other cities. With my connections through Captain Tony along with my various other hustles, it was almost too easy for me to slide into the world of dealing. As long as I kept a low profile and didn't flaunt my trafficking, I managed to stay off the police radar.

Other rookie dealers weren't so discreet, unfortunately. I saw guys show up driving shiny new sports cars, flashing money around, and acting like they owned Duval Street. Those were the ones who got busted quickly.

I tried to be smarter—I used a day job doing fishing charters as cover. Several week-long fishing trips to the Tortugas kept me legitimate due to the reputation as first mate for Captain Andy Griffith Sr. At the beginning, I was just looking to hook up friends and make a little extra cash. I went with Sal when he gave Tennessee Williams a mask for his house and Tennessee asked me if I could get him some of that famous Key West white powder, which I did, of course.

Drugs were such a part of the culture that we'd do drugs just for the sake of doing drugs. For instance, there was a time when a lot of quaaludes were coming in through Key West and the Florida Keys. Bags of chips and powder parachuted down bundled in special cushioned wooden crates, sometimes hitting land and sometimes ending up in the water. It wasn't marketable at all except maybe to some friends for a party. But because it was just showing up we had to figure out something to do with it, hence quaalude tea. We'd mix a teaspoon or two with some nice green tea and lots of honey and drink while hot. It still tasted bad but it would knock the shit out of you much quicker than if you took a pill. Everybody was doing that for about a year and a half.

I started getting more involved in bigger deals. One went bad and I got robbed at gunpoint for 20 grand. I lost the money but thankfully not my life. Instead of getting out of the business, I started packing a pistol, which was probably the wrong direction to go. But those Miami boys were also packing—I wasn't about to get caught unprepared again. Making money off all that tourist demand started to feel more dangerous than it was worth.

By the late '70s, tastes were changing from pot to harder drugs, and the influx of coke made people even more brazen: the big money brought bigger egos and bigger risks. Guys like my buddy Mike had mastered smuggling routes from Colombia and became rich overnight. He drove a new Caddy, owned a speedboat, and didn't think twice about buying rounds of Dom Perignon for everyone at Captain Tony's, just because we could. It was almost like he was asking to get busted. I tried to avoid the excesses of the blow scene, but eventually got pulled in deeper.

The infamous Fire Chief Bum Farto before his mysterious disappearance.

6

FROM THE HIGHEST OF HIGHS . . .

The first time I saw Lisa in 1979 I was cycling to work. I immediately parked my bike and went over to introduxce myself. She was stunning. I said hi and she replied in the most heavenly Georgia belle accent—my heart instantly turned to butter. As our small talk progressed, I found out she was 17. That was probably why she was turning down my invitation for her to visit Captain Tony's Saloon during my next shift. I honestly don't remember if I was playing the long game or if I was just flirting when I asked if I could take her out when she turned 18. Regardless, she responded immediately.

"Why don't you take me out now?"

Our first date was at Port of Call, the fanciest place on the island. I desperately wanted to impress this stunning model and embarrassingly couldn't pronounce half the items on the menu. We started meeting for every sunset and I knew I had to clear the field of all the other girls I was dating. I was ready for something real.

The following weeks included bikini-clad photo shoots, sandbar trips, partying, and the natural high of lust-fueled new love; we were falling hard for each other. Lisa knew I had a darker side and secretly she loved dipping her toes in that world.

1980 Lisa Jo Burke during a shoot for the Dale Wittner agency at the Casa Marina. Photos by Keith Tarracina

Meeting Lisa was one of the best things that ever happened to me. I was over the moon when she moved into my place on Seminary Street. My grandfather loved her too and got her a fake ID so she could work as a bartender at Captain Tony's Saloon. We were inseparable. Lisa's youthful passion and zest for life lit me up inside. I loved showing her all my favorite spots and watching her marvel at the island's beauty with fresh eyes. Her innocence and kindness balanced out my edge and troublemaking side. Even though I still partied hard I felt like I had everything under control.

Life was beautiful for both of us so we decided to move to an amazing Conch house on Elgin Lane with the entire bottom floor 3-bedroom apartment all to ourselves and I asked Lisa's mom, Cecilia, to move into the back bedroom. Our landlord Freddie was an experienced sailor and occasionally went on runs to Cuba with Captain Tony. For over a year we had great times: great cooking, fantastic parties, and everything else paradise could offer.

Keith West original sunset from Simonton st pier right next to the famous beach bar Lagerheads 1979

The author Shel Silverstein had become a very good friend of mine. I met him in 1978 and he bought a beautiful house on the island in 1980. Lisa and I were frequent guests there, even having Thanksgiving with him one year.

I was photographing Lisa and other models for the Dale Whitner Advertising Agency. Shel saw some of Lisa's bikini pics and told me he could easily get her in Playboy Magazine. He'd been doing cartoons for them since the 1960s and was good friends with Hugh Hefner. He offered to send in the proofs and arrange a shoot.

I kept my cool on the outside but inside I was seething. As an Italian guy from Jersey, *nobody* was going to see *my* girl naked. I just shrugged off the offer with, "I don't think so."

Shel pressed on.

"She'll get paid a lot of money. It'll be fun! You can fly there, too!"

I finally snapped.

"No! It ain't happenin'!"

Lisa and I did talk about it later and she left it up to me. But there was no changing my mind. Shel was just trying to be helpful and we laughed about that exchange many times over the years. We remained close friends and his passing was a great loss for me.

Things are going pretty well when your biggest problem is deciding whether or not your girlfriend should do a Playboy pictorial. My dream life in paradise was pretty nice.

However, somewhere along the way, I started to take Lisa

for granted. The spark faded as we transitioned from the honeymoon phase into a more real, mature relationship. When Cecilia was single, she was almost invisible, quietly going about her life. But with her boyfriend Ricky, their presence was constant, and our carefree romance started to feel like a mundane family routine. Although I genuinely liked Ricky and had no issue with him moving in after just a month of dating Lisa's mom, having another couple in the house somehow altered the entire dynamic.

My eye started to wander again at the bar with all the flirty, carefree tourists looking to have fun and experiment while on vacation. I thought Lisa was too wholesome and naive for the scene I was part of with all the booze, drugs, and sex. The temptations were just too strong and I shamefully broke it off with her to pursue the temptations of the island .

Of course, Lisa was shocked and heartbroken. I was racked with guilt but still too immature and selfish at the time to really feel the depth of what I had thrown away. Because the only comfort I could find was in the thick of the action on my post at the door of Captain Tony's Saloon, I reacted by partying even harder and fully embracing the wild, seedy side of Key West that I had only dabbled in while I was with Lisa.

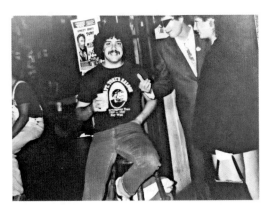

The command stool, here I regulated the bar for my grandfather and kept my hand on the pulse of the island

I was devastated but had only myself to blame. Over the next months, I desperately tried forgetting Lisa by chasing even more women and getting deeper into the drug and party scene. My life grew emptier even as it looked glitzier on the surface.

Key West graveyard with the Atlantic ocean in the background of this flyover photo taken by Keith Terracina 1981

7

TO THE LOWEST OF LOWS

This is the story of one person I knew but it's happened to thousands: the curse of Key West.

I became friends with a man who had a successful business in Chicago. He came down to Key West with his wife and two daughters for a vacation in paradise. They stayed at a nice hotel, rode the Conch Train, and enjoyed the best restaurants and bars, even meeting Captain Tony and other local business owners.

Back in Chicago the couple realized it was too straightlaced for them—at leasts for him, anyway.. Family life is stifling. They split and within a few months the husband filed for divorce. He made sure his ex and his kids are taken care of and he moved to Key West. The locals he'd talk to on vacation seemed to be living the dream. He wanted that, too.

This man opened a restaurant. It did alright and he was making a comfortable living: he wasn't getting rich but it supported his lifestyle. Some of his friends from up

North started visiting and realized he could hook them up with weed, coke, or whatever they needed because he had connections. This became the guy's side hustle. He was partying, drinking, doing lots of coke and welcoming a steady stream of friends and friends of friends coming South for fun in the sun. The restaurant really started rolling and he was living it up.

The curse had struck. He's in the Key West corner of the Bermuda Triangle. There's only one way it can go from there.

My friend met a girl. They were getting high together and having fun. Then she cheated on him. He got upset and started neglecting the restaurant, freebasing and drinking like crazy.

Within two years, he lost the restaurant. In an attempt to cover some of his debt, he sold the house that the wife and daughters were living in back in Chicago without telling her. He also lost his cute little house in Key West.

I know it happens everywhere but it's become a cliché in Key West: you think you've caught your dream but it slips through your fingers and you're left with nothing.

Without Lisa's positive, stabilizing influence in my life, I started going off the rails. The once sleepy, peaceful island was seeing more violent crime, harder drugs, and just an overall edgier energy as tourism exploded. Key West was taking a turn and I went with it. In 1981, I became a smuggler.

For as long as shipping lanes connecting Europe and the Americas intersected with places like Cuba, the Bahamas, and the Dry Tortugas, Key West was a place to rest, restock, make deals, and party. It's always been a smuggler's town. Whatever contraband was in transit, some of it ended up there.

In 1982, Peruvian Flake hit the island. It was by far the best cocaine on planet Earth, even better than Bolivian Rock. It was pinkish with a sheen and it melted in your hand. It looked like pink diamonds when light hit it. Whatever they cut it with was neutral or there was no cutting at all. You could have great sex with other cokes but also have some problems. Not with Peruvian Flake: you felt like Superman,

You could be at Studio 54. You could be at the Palladium. You could be at the best clubs in Miami. Everybody had coke. But if you had Peruvian Flake you were special; you ruled the world. You could get in with movie stars, millionaires, billionaires, anyone. Doors opened up because not everybody had access to it. Money controls people but Peruvian Flake controlled the people with the money.

I was a good photographer but that's not why a lot of my pictures were published: I knew the people who had Peruvian Flake. That's why I had so many posters and postcards printed. I met lots of rich friends through my grandfather; I kept them because I could get Peruvian Flake.

My buddy Mike was still thriving as a smuggler and I partnered with him. We came up with a code for ordering drugs over our phones in case any agencies had tapped us. We used lobster for weed and shrimp for cocaine. After closing up the bar one night, I was in a rush to call Mike to order up some favors for a crew coming in from Miami the next day. I mistakenly called my other buddy Mike who was a deputy sheriff. The blood drained from my face when the wrong Mike pulled up on the sidewalk in his sheriff's department cruiser and yelled, "Get your 20 pounds of lobster, yet?!"

He was laughing but his tone was still serious. I froze in the doorway for what seemed like an eternity but could only have been a few seconds as I realized I'd called the wrong Mike. I was still a small-timer and while our friendship had probably earned me a little leeway from Sheriff's Deputy Mike, the bottom line was that I was not worth his time. Still, he had sent me a not-so-subtle warning that I should be more careful.

Of course, I knew there were major players on the island doing way bigger deals than mine. I had seen it firsthand one day down at the docks in the year before after the biggest marijuana bust in Key West history. In 1981, the DEA had seized a freighter just offshore with 200 tons of Panama Red onboard—hundreds of bales ready for distribution up and down the East Coast .

First photographer on scene at the largest drug seizure in Florida, 200 tons of Panama Red. Photo Keith Terracina 1981

By this time I was the staff photographer for the local paper, the Key West Citizen. Roger Bartell, the managing editor, called me early in the morning and sent me to the Navy base to cover the seizure. I was the first photographer on site. The local authorities had a special "work release" for county prisoners to help unload the cargo. Each 90-pound bale had to be cut open and a sample was taken out to be put into a baggie.

The police chief just wanted it quietly sent away to be incinerated—he didn't want to scare off the tourists with bad PR. Five moving trucks were packed with premium weed that was to be disposed of up the keys. Interestingly, only four trucks showed up at the incinerator. The fifth was never accounted for. Not the most ethical police work, but that's how the Bubba system operated. As long as the party continued uninterrupted, law and order took a back seat, Key West style.

My pictures were in newspapers throughout Florida and made it into High Times Magazine. The weed may have had an even broader distribution. Not only did a truck go missing but the freighter had been carrying a lot more than 200 tons. Before it had been intercepted, a lot of cargo had been offloaded to five shrimp boats. Once they were clear of the freighter they offloaded to smaller boats that scattered. With the Navy, Coast Guard, and DEA looking for smugglers, some captains panicked and started dumping bales. Once Panama Red started washing up in the mangroves, everyone went fishing. Kids were skipping school. There was not one boat in a marina from Key West to Key Largo.

Everyone on the island had a stash of Panama Red. Garbage cans were stuffed with it. Local entrepreneurs saw an opportunity to profit by selling their surplus but they couldn't get it off the island. There were roadblocks in and out of Key West. That's what kicked off the Conch Rebellion with the Conch Republic being established the following year.

When Key West seceded in April 1982—declaring war, surrendering, and requesting one billion dollars in foreign aid all in just over a minute—it was a great tourism ploy but it also highlighted the impact of the long federal lockdown of Highway 1 from Key Largo to Key West. During this drug drought in 1982, I became emboldened by my local reputation and decided to try and finesse a large deal out of a new connection through my new friend Ronnie. He claimed to have some great Columbian connections in Miami. The deal was for me to buy several bales. In Key West, we would always take the burlap and packaging weight off the price but when I brought this up to these new drug runners they started to get fidgety. The language barrier amplified tensions so I attempted to de-escalate the situation by splitting the difference but this set the Columbians off even further. I agreed to their terms just to get out of there and back to my friends in the hotel awaiting their score.

Most of the deals with Ronnie worked out but he could also be careless. Alarm bells should have gone off in my head when Ronnie called to ask for a pound of cocaine for his friends from San Francisco. He never had any money and was always desperate for another score so I should have known something was off. I grilled him up and down if he really knew these guys and he swore that he did.

I was super 24/7 paranoid from doing quaaludes to keep the edge off the Peruvian flake but I figured I'd least have a meeting. I can't use the bar because Captain Tony would have kicked my ass so I arranged to see the buyers at The Bull on Duval Street. We got a table and I told them that they were safe with me: this was my island. Since I didn't know them, I needed them to show me their driver's licenses before I could hook them up.

They pulled out the shiniest brand-new plastic IDs I'd ever seen. Clearly they were DEA or undercover agents. I nodded approvingly and said we'd meet up again in an hour: I had no intention of ever seeing them again.

I left and immediately called Ronnie to tell him that I was out. He still thought the deal was solid and wanted to take them to Miami. He was confident he could score what they wanted. That was the last time I spoke to him. I do know his landlord was still looking for him months later.

I set up shop at 704 Caroline Street and that became my Den of Sin. I had a huge credit line with many of the dealers in Key West so they would front me product anytime I wanted it. I could then cut it to feed my own habit but a lot of the time the product was so weak buyers thought I was selling them baking soda—sometimes I wasn't. My cutting cost me my reputation as the Coke King of Key West.

My downward spiral continued as I borrowed more and more money to pay off my other debts. Wally, an investor from Jersey, heard that I had the hookup on shrimp and he had money to invest so we all sat down with Capitan Tony and discussed opening a restaurant on the side of the bar. Wally paid my grandfather $18,000 upfront in rent. Our restaurant was an immediate success. All of my creditors started to leave me alone once they saw the restaurant was doing well.

Since I appeared to have everything under control, Wally took a trip back to Jersey. With him gone, I started taking on other partners and gave them each a 20% stake: the catch was that none of them knew about each other. Wally noticed that the deposits stopped going into the restaurant's bank account and he got suspicious of me but I had a way of convincing him that everything was fine. I leaned on him and told him I was reinvesting the profits and he dropped it. He didn't know about my seedy dark side so I was able to stretch this scheme out for about two months.

As this dragged on and my financial situation got worse and worse, I told Wally I had to pay some other debts. The poor guy kept trusting me. I was skimming off the restaurant because I couldn't borrow money anywhere else: no one believed my song and dance about a big shipment coming in anymore.

I was desperate for a big score and I was running out of time. With my debt and everything around me swirling out of control I knew I had limited opportunities to put anything together. I heard about some guys from Alabama who were looking for cocaine so I reached out. I assured them I had a big deal coming down if they could just front me five grand.

Delivering heavily cut coke was a mistake.

After my clients sampled my product, they called and demanded I meet them at the Raw Bar. We talked in their car for a minute as I explained I didn't have their money and needed time to get it. Not satisfied that they had made it clear how upset they were, they drove me up to Big Coppitt—less than 10 miles up the Keys—and let me out of the car with my hands tied before beating me. They worked the ribs and stomach until I threw up. Then they drove off.

I stumbled back to the main road and hitchhiked home with cracked ribs and a bloody mouth from the tooth they knocked out. I knew they weren't done with me. They hadn't finished me off because there was a chance I'd pay them back. But if they ever suspected that I was going to stiff them, I'd be shark bait.

I needed a score and fast.

My only play was to tell one of my long-time customers that I was short $20,000 for my smuggler's deposit on some incredible uncut kilos but if he gave me $5,000 I'd give him all his money back plus some coke. It worked and I was able to pay off the Alabama guys the next day and avoid becoming chum.

While that took care of one problem, it was just part of the much bigger mess my life had become. Two days later my ticket would get punched again when two old school Conch Cuban's that I owed $8,000 to pulled up to get their money. I tried to buy time but none of my typical bullshit stories would work on these old timers. They drove me across the island to an old Conch neighborhood and sat me down. They gave me an opportunity to make a phone call and get the money because they thought I had property in Jersey. They were not playing around but only smacked me around a little.

I had 24 hours to get the money or I was going back on the sharks' menu. My new scheme was to convince the girl I was staying with that we should sell her Bronco. As soon as she handed over the pink slip I traded it to the Cubans to square my debt.

After a couple weeks of couch surfing and freebasing, I came to the realization one day that my small island world was crashing down on me from every direction. Everyone that I owed money to was talking to each other. They were showing up at my friends' houses. I kept thinking that someone would front me enough money that I could come into a big score that would allow me to cut enough product to pay all my debts. The crippling depression I was in from my collapsing life would not allow me to stop freebasing or I would have immediately contemplated ending my story.

The next day I called up Double Raft Donnie and asked for him to come pick me up. I had about ten base hits ready with me and slunk down in the backseat to avoid being seen. Donnie had been in prison for two years and didn't know how bad I had gotten until that day. One look at me and he knew the whole story. He brought me to Key West when we were both ready to take on the world; now he was sneaking me out cowering in his backseat.

I didn't even make it to Big Coppitt before I had to take

another hit. I smoked all the way to Islamorada where my buddy Roy Smith lived on a houseboat. I was so paranoid I was worried about being spotted by the rest of the people I owed money to even all the way up there at MM 88.

I couldn't stop pacing. I didn't even want to go inside. I knew I had to call Captain Tony's and check-in. I called and Lisa's friend Debbie answered. She was ecstatic to hear from me. I told her to tell everyone I was in Miami doing some deals and that I'd be back in a few weeks.

Lisa had come back to Key West two months earlier and jumped into the bartending circuit. She had seen me working my shady dealings around town and had heard the salt associated with my name. She was at Captain Tony's and grabbed the phone from Debbie.

"What the hell did you do, Keith?"

Lisa already knew what was going on. Hearing the anger and disappointment in her voice hurt more than anything else I'd been through. I wanted her to trust me again, to believe me. That was my new dream. I thought I could keep it alive with a lie.

"It's nothing. I've just gotta take care of this thing in Miami and then I'll be back. In a few weeks."

After a brief stay with Roy we went to Miami so I could catch a flight to Ohio and stay with my buddy from the newspaper, Roger Bartell. He put me up until I got my head together and moved back home to Elizabeth, New Jersey. I finally had to face the music of how far I had fallen.

8

A NARROW ESCAPE

That first year up North was far from glamorous. The nonstop sunshine was replaced by gray skies and frigid blasts of winter air. I traded island living for a dingy apartment in a rough part of Elizabeth. My fancy photography gigs were replaced by boring department store portraits. I learned quickly that big-city customers lacked the patience of all those happy vacationers lining up for photos back in Key West.

All of this was compounded by the lingering depression that came from withdrawing from the daily cocktail of intoxicants that fueled my life in the Keys. Sobriety made it painfully clear how much I took that lifestyle for granted. I now had to earn an honest living and endure awful weather merely to afford a fraction of the leisure I'd enjoyed basking in paradise. But it also gave me the perspective and the determination to build a new life without looking over my shoulder.

In time, the haze lifted and I began regaining my

confidence and ambition. I started bonding with customers over our shared experiences rather than just rushing through sessions impatiently. Business picked up as I invested more creativity into photography and made connections around town. Before long I was known as the guy for family portraits and graduation photos as my unique style stood out from the competition.

As business grew steadily, I expanded by hiring assistants and purchasing a storefront location. My wild past started fading into memory as I focused on doing honest work and staying on the straight and narrow. Things really turned around when I began getting calls for magazine gigs and fashion shoots in addition to my studio work. Soon I was able to purchase a nice home in the peaceful suburbs where I finally felt at ease again.

Be careful speeding in the fast lane of the Key West party scene with no seat belt on.

Looking back now, I lived enough crazy adventures for several lifetimes. My rollercoaster seven years in Key West were unforgettable, though much of it seems like a surreal dream. I'm grateful for the perspective my exile gave me along with the second chance to build a rewarding career. Things could easily have gone sideways and landed me locked up or in an early grave like so many of my old running buddies. Temptation undoubtedly awaits around the next corner. But the wisdom of age reminds me there are no shortcuts without consequences. For now, I'll enjoy the fruits of my hard labor and leave the danger to the reckless youth.

9

IT'S STILL PARADISE

Sitting here now in my 60s, I can't help but feel tremendously grateful for the extraordinary life I've been blessed to live. While there have certainly been highs and lows along the way, the time in Key West stands out as magical.

The star of the famous cat man show at Mallory Square. Rumor has it that he'll be back in 2 weeks. Keith Terracina 1981.

That blissful slice of time, when I was still just a wide-eyed kid in my early 20s, shaped me profoundly and awakened me to wondrous possibilities I'd never imagined back home in Elizabeth, New Jersey. Although four decades have passed since those halcyon days, hardly a week goes by when my mind doesn't wander back to the people, places, and moments that made the Key West of the 1970s the way it was.

Whenever I return to Key West these days, I still catch glimpses of the past if I know where to look. Turning down Duval Street on my bike, I'll spot a familiar face that transports me back in time. Or I'll notice a street performer trying out some fire juggling tricks similar to the ones I watched Will Soto perfect all those years ago at Mallory Square . Occasionally, I even get a whiff of someone smoking a joint furtively in an alleyway, proving some local traditions never change.

Here Will Soto amazes generations of visitors with his outstanding balance and juggling skills. Keith Terracina 1978

Mostly though, it's a feeling I get walking the streets of
Old Town after dark, with the salty air kissing my skin—that
the spirits of yesterday still linger, suspended in time. More
than once, I could swear I spotted the mischievous specter
of good ol' Captain Tony himself, keeping watch over his
island paradise with a Lucky Strike dangling from his lips
and a twinkle in his eye.

Rest in Paradise Capitan

Little Tony and her beloved father stop to pose during another crazy night at the saloon in the early 80's.

Of course, many of the folks I caroused with during Key West's "anything goes" heyday are no longer with us. Sadly, some passed away before their time due to hard living, while others simply faded from memory after our paths diverged. For decades, I wondered what became of Peter the manager, Big Al, Boat Bar Charlie, and so many more who indelibly shaped my coming-of-age during that wild epoch.

There was one person in particular whose fate weighed heavily on my mind over the years—my first real love, Lisa. After I snuck out of Key West, I figured I'd never lay eyes on her again. For decades, her memory lingered stubbornly in the recesses of my mind as the one that got away.

That's why out of the blue eight years ago, when a Facebook friend request from a "Lisa Jo Burke" popped up, I practically fell out of my chair. Could it really be her after all this time? I hesitantly sent a message asking if it was her. Moments later came the stunning confirmation that Lisa and I had found each other again. Time stopped.

We must have talked on the phone for three hours that night, reminiscing about old times and catching up on everything that had transpired in the nearly 40 years since we'd last seen each other. I confessed how I'd often thought of her fondly over the decades and expressed my deepest regrets for how terribly things ended between us.

Ever the kind soul I remembered, she immediately accepted my apology and said dwelling on the past would be silly at our age. The warmth, affection, and ease of our conversation made it feel like no time had passed at all. We were giddy kids again, swept up in nostalgia.

From then on, hardly a day went by that we didn't speak— sometimes for hours on end. The more we opened up, the clearer it became that the powerful connection between us still crackled as intensely as ever. Before a month went by, I'd booked a flight to Orlando where Lisa had lived for years.

Stepping off the plane at the airport going to Orlando, butterflies swirled in my stomach just like when I first laid eyes on her all those years before. As soon as I spotted her waiting by the baggage claim, that familiar electricity passed between us, leaving no doubt that our bond was unbreakable. We embraced tenderly, the lost time vanishing in an instant.

Taking Lisa's hand in mine, I turned to her and asked if we should go home. Four months later, I relocated permanently to Orlando.

Getting to know this new version of Lisa—so much wiser and yet still the same soul I'd fallen for long ago—felt like the greatest stroke of good fortune imaginable. Watching movies together while nestled on the couch, taking midnight strolls hand-in-hand under the stars, cooking dinner side-by-side in her cozy kitchen—even the simplest pleasures thrilled me to no end.

Her elegant beauty and kindhearted spirit were just as I remembered. And any lingering guilt I held over past mistakes dissolved completely when Lisa assured me that she, too, had made peace with our turbulent history ages ago. The only thing that mattered, she insisted while squeezing my hand tenderly, was sharing each new day together going forward. I couldn't agree more. Who would have thought that after all the twists and turns over so many years, Lisa and I would reunite to revive the easy rhythm we once knew so well, older and wiser but still as hopelessly smitten as ever? I suppose it's true what they say—every end is merely a prelude to a new beginning .

Cheers to the star crossed lovers, no matter how far they roam.

Now comfortably retired, we've settled into a charmed life as snowbirds, splitting time between Altamonte Springs outside Orlando and my beloved Key West. Every time we set foot on the island, it feels like coming home again. Meandering aimlessly through Old Town with no particular place to be, I'm filled with profound gratitude for this second act in life's great play.

As for dear old Captain Tony, the man responsible for originally bringing me down to Key West all those years ago, his larger-than-life aura still permeates the island. When he finally passed away at age 93 back in 2008, the legendary saloon keeper owed over $2 million and hadn't paid taxes in decades. But no one seemed to mind since Tony was considered local royalty, having put wild and wonderful Key West on the map for so many visitors over the years.

Fittingly, his good buddy, the late Jimmy Buffett. wrote a song immortalizing Tony called "Last Mango in Paris" and even mentions their friendship in his final song, "Bubble's Up." Captain Tony sold the saloon when he became mayor of Key West in 1989—yes, that happened—but it retains much of the same character. In fact, his boisterous spirit remains forever woven into the island's cultural fabric .

Legend has it that some of Jimmy Buffet's friends provided the swing votes to get Tony elected.

My Great Uncle Sal and Tennessee Williams would throw parties in the upstairs studio or at Tennessee's house and fill them with attractive young men. The morning after their parties they'd hang out in Captain Tony's with my grandfather and Peter talking about the night before or their old adventures in New York or Cuba before Castro. Often, I'd get a call to pick up something like hot Cuban bread, espressos, or some sandwiches. I'd show up with whatever they'd ordered and Sal would be chomping on his cigar while Tennessee would be rolling with laughter at whatever I'd just missed .

Everyone always had a blast at those late morning breakfasts. I just sat and listened. I felt like I had nothing that stacked up to their stories that flew back and forth. Once—in the middle of some epic tale—my Great Uncle Sal stopped, pointed to me and said the name only he ever used, "Keet is going to tell the story, the *real* story, of all of us. Many years from now. *He's* going to be the one."

I never knew what he was talking about until 20 years ago. When I inherited his estate of photography and all the Key West glass slides I finally understood that those memories had to be shared and that it was my responsibility to do it. I also realized my own adventures belong in the collection. Shel Silverstein told me to write them all down and I do what Shel says. Sometimes.

The Key West bottle wall stood for over 20 years and became an iconic part of Key West's landscape until 91 when it was taken down by Carolyn